T0047137

COMMUNITIES OF RESISTANCE AND PREFIGURATIVE POLITICS

THE AQUINAS LECTURE, 2023

COMMUNITIES OF RESISTANCE AND PREFIGURATIVE POLITICS

JOSÉ MEDINA

MARQUETTE
UNIVERSITY
PRESS

The Aquinas Lectures
Under the auspices of the
Wisconsin-Alpha Chapter of Phi Sigma Tau

Library of Congress Cataloging-in-Publication Data

Names: Medina, José, 1968- author.
Title: Communities of resistance and prefigurative politics / José Medina.
Description: First Edition. | Milwaukee, WI : Marquette University Press,
 [2023] | Series: The Aquinas lecture; 85 | Includes bibliographical
 references. | Summary: "Communal practices of resistance and protest can
 be understood as prefiguration or the performative anticipation of
 social change, that resisting oppression requires participating in a
 community of resistance whose counter-practices abolish unjust social
 arrangements and engages in alternative world-making, prefiguring
 alternative futures, and more just societies"-- Provided by publisher.
Identifiers: LCCN 2023035414 | ISBN 9781626001008 (cloth)
Subjects: LCSH: Social movements. | Government, Resistance to. | Social
 change. | Social justice.
Classification: LCC HM881 .M4353 2023 | DDC 303.48/4--dcedtf
LC record available at https://lccn.loc.gov/2023035414

ASSOCIATION
of UNIVERSITY
PRESSES

The Philosophy Department of Marquette University on behalf of Phi Sigma Tau, the Philosophy Honors Society, each year invites a scholar to deliver a lecture in honor of St. Thomas Aquinas.

José Medina

The 2023 Aquinas Lecture, *Communities of Resistance and Prefigurative Politics* was delivered on Friday, October 6, 2023, by José Medina.

Dr. José Medina is Walter Dill Scott Professor of Philosophy at Northwestern University, with affiliations in African American Studies, Gender and Sexuality Studies, and the Spanish and Portuguese Department. He received his B.A in

Philosophy from the University of Sevilla, his M.A. in Philosophy from Northwestern University, and his PhD in Philosophy from Northwestern University. His primary fields of expertise are critical philosophy of race, feminist and queer theory, social epistemology, and political philosophy.

Medina has published five monographs, five edited (or co-edited) volumes, and over seventy articles and book chapters. His latest book, *The Epistemology of Protest: Silencing, Epistemic Activism, and the Communicative Life of Resistance*, came out with Oxford University Press in 2023. Previous books include *The Epistemology of Resistance: Gender and Racial Oppression, Epistemic Injustice, and Resistant Imaginations* (Oxford University Press, 2013), recipient of the North-American Society for Social Philosophy Book Award.

His current projects focus on how social perception and the social imagination contribute to the formation of vulnerabilities to different kinds of violence and oppression. These projects also explore the social movements and kinds of activism (including what he terms "epistemic activism") that can be mobilized to resist racial and sexual violence and oppression in local and global contexts. Current book projects on theories of oppression and resistance include the collection of essays *Resistance* for Oxford University Press.

To Professor Medina's distinguished list of publications, the Philosophy Department and Phi Sigma Tau are pleased to add: *Communities of Resistance and Prefigurative Politics.*

COMMUNITIES OF RESISTANCE AND PREFIGURATIVE POLITICS

JOSÉ MEDINA

WALTER DILL SCOTT PROFESSOR OF PHILOSOPHY NORTHWESTERN UNIVERSITY

Resisting recalcitrant forms of injustice (such as racism, sexism, homophobia, transphobia, etc.) is not an easy thing to do. It requires overcoming social silences along with other communicative and epistemic obstacles. It also requires social mobilization and the creation of a protesting public or community of resistance in which protesting voices can flourish and resistors can help each other to survive experiences of injustice and work toward a world without injustice. *Protesting* injustice is precisely the kind of communicative activity that enables resistant subjects and communities to do that.

In the first section of this essay, I lay out an account of *protest* as a communicative mechanism for the creation of protesting publics or communities of resistance that makes it possible to break silences and overcome communicative and epistemic injustices that exist under conditions of oppression. Drawing from my latest book *The Epistemology of Protest,*[1] I argue against narrow conceptions of protest as an instrument of public persuasion, and I argue that the primary function of protest is to create a community of resistance or protesting public. Building on that account, in the second section I elucidate the subversive potential of the counter-cultures and resistant imaginations developed by communities of resistance. In particular, I argue that communal practices of resistance should be understood as *prefiguration,* or the performative anticipation of social change. Connecting queer theory and queer activism with the neo-Marxist literature on prefiguration and counter-communities, I discuss acts of resistance as a performative mechanism of prefigurative politics, showing how protest actions enable resistors to anticipate in their actions the social world that they want to bring about. Finally, in section three, drawing from women of color feminist scholarship, I discuss how resistant imaginations

1 Medina, José. *The Epistemology of Protest: Silencing, Epistemic Activism, and the Communicative Life of Protest* (New York: Oxford University Press, 2023).

function in protest actions both (a) as a way of protesting and opposing injustices, and (b) as a way of transforming the world and transforming ourselves through alternative world- making (world-disclosure or prefiguration). Resistant imaginations become embodied and alive in the subversive practices of communities of resistance that performatively prefigure the possibility of a world without injustice. It is through the defiant lives and actions of communities of resistance that counter-imaginations can performatively anticipate alternative worlds. In this concluding section, I elucidate how resistant imaginations operate in action in counter-communal practices of resistance, focusing especially on what Asha Bhandary calls "living counterfactually"[2] and what Saidiya Hartman has described as the "beautiful experiments of living" of "riotous black girls" and "queer radicals."[3]

---

2 Bhandary, Asha Leena. "Caring for Whom? Racial Practices of Care and Liberal Constructivism" *Philosophies* 7 no. 4: 78 (July 2022) 1-14; https://doi.org/10.3390/philosophies7040078.

3 Hartman, Saidiya. *Wayward Lives, Beautiful Experiments: Intimate Histories of Riotous Black Girls, Troublesome Women, and Queer Radicals* (New York: Norton, 2019).

1. PROTEST AS A MECHANISM
OF PUBLIC FORMATION

Drawing from Judith Butler's performative theory of assembly,[4] in this section I argue for a conception of protest as a communicative mechanism that performatively creates the possibility of a resistant public and makes space for resistance. The argument for this view of protest is developed in two steps: firstly, by engaging critically with the literature on protest and carving the space for a performative account of protest as a mechanism of social change (1.a); and secondly, by sketching an account of how protest acts can performatively constitute communities of resistance and performatively *prefigure* the possibility of a world without injustice (1.b). The central aim of the argument in this section is to show that the primary function of protest is creating and sustaining communities of resistance (rather than "informing and persuading the general public," as traditionally understood).

---

4 See Butler, Judith. *Notes toward a Performative Theory of Assembly* (Cambridge, MA: Harvard University Press, 2015).

1. A. BEYOND THE INSTRUMENTAL VIEW OF PROTEST AND TOWARD A PERFORMATIVE VIEW.

In the *Epistemology of Protest*,[5] I developed an account of protest under conditions of oppression and argued against two widespread misconceptions about protest: that protesting is an easy thing to do in Western liberal democracies with *formal* freedoms of assembly and expression, and that protest has epistemic value only as an *instrument* of public information and persuasion. Against these assumptions, the *Epistemology of Protest* argues that (1) it is not easy for people to come to protest even in democratic societies because it requires a difficult process of critical awakening about experiences of injustice and overcoming communicative and epistemic challenges against speaking up posed by oppressive conditions, and (2) protesting has *intrinsic* communicative and epistemic value that goes beyond informing and persuading others and consists in transforming the public sphere by creating new publics and attempting to transform social sensibilities.

One of the misconceptions about protest that I have tried to debunk is that when freedoms of assembly and expression are *formally* conferred by

---

5 Medina *The Epistemology of Protest: Silencing, Epistemic Activism, and the Communicative Life of Protest,* 2023.

law, *everyone* can enter the public sphere to protest and *everyone* is ready and willing to listen to their protest. Unfortunately, forms of oppression and marginalization (such as classism, racism, sexism, homophobia, and transphobia), which have been and continue to be pervasive in society—including Western democratic societies—make it very difficult for certain groups to become constituted as a protesting public, to express themselves, and to secure proper uptake for their protests.

Unfortunately, it has not been easy for all protesting voices to carry weight in public life, to command communicative respect and attention, to be considered seriously and without prejudices. Of course, it does make a very important difference to have democratic freedoms formally guaranteed, for the struggles of oppressed protesting publics can then happen (for the most part, at least) in the open, as part of the communicative life of the public sphere, without having to go underground and remain relegated to a clandestine political world. Yet, the view that in Western liberal democracies everyone can protest freely and be heard is simply not true. This naive, self-congratulatory view that often circulates in academia and in public life hides the important fact that even when the right to protest is not formally and *de jure* curtailed, it is often practically and *de facto* constrained by different forms of communicative and epistemic marginalization. Liberation movements know this well, and a key component of the struggles for liberation of movements such as abolitionism, the women's movement, or the queer movement is precisely fighting against communicative and epistemic challenges in order to become visible, to have a voice, and to have their perspectives properly heard and considered. As the communicative and epistemic struggles of liberation movements show, protesting can be a hard and difficult achievement even in democratic societies, requiring the development of new communicative attitudes and habits as well as new democratic practices and relations that expand formal rights and make the public sphere more inclusive.

Another misconception about protest that I have tried to debunk is the idea that what defines a protest is that there is a clear message that a protesting public delivers to a particular audience that is already there, ready to listen. On this picture, protest has epistemic value only as an *instrument* of public information and persuasion. Protest is depicted as a communicative and epistemic mechanism through which a protesting public informs, and if successful, persuades the general public and the institutions about something or other that they are protesting. I reject this instrumental view of protest for several reasons. I propose an alternative, non-instrumental view of

protest according to which a protest is to be val-
ued not just as a communicative and epistemic
instrument, but as a communicative and epistemic
process of collective learning and discovery. On my
view, protest does not simply have instrumental
value because of the communicative and epistemic
goods that it can deliver. Protest has intrinsic
communicative and epistemic value because of the
kind of activity that it is: participating in protest
is engaging in a process of collective learning, a
process of learning about experiences of injustices
and a process of envisioning together a more just
world. Through protest a public can develop and
exercise collective epistemic agency that can produce group testimony, new forms of understanding, critical visions, and collective imaginings.

Let me highlight some of the crucial points
that the instrumental view of protest misses. In
the first place, the full complexity and transformative potential of the communicative activity of
protesting is missed if a protest is conceived as the
delivery of a fully formed message by a previously
existing collective subject or public. This picture misses that protest involves a *process of subject constitution*: it is in and through protest that
the collective identity of a protesting public gets
constituted or re-constituted. This picture also
misses that protest involves a *process of articulation*
of new understandings and new critical insights

and visions: it is in and through protest that publics shape their perspectives and elaborate their critical insights.

Moreover, as I will discuss in the next two sections, it is through protesting acts and practices of resistance that counter-communities can change the world, that they can engage in alternative world-making and performatively *prefigure* new forms of sociality and a more just world.

In the second place, the instrumental view also misses that a protest is a complex communicative process that can be characterized as an open address that is always *in search of an audience*. Protests *prefigure* their audiences whether they are there or not, and they contain communicative and epistemic efforts to reshape existing audiences or to create new ones. It is not uncommon to find protesting voices addressing future generations, or simply communicative or epistemic versions of ourselves that are different from the way we are currently constituted as hearers and knowers and the way we are prepared (or unprepared) to listen. In short, protest has the power to change available forms of communicative receptivity and to generate new forms of sensibility. Protests can create new audiences or transform existing ones. This leads directly to the last point that I want to highlight regarding what the instrumental view of protest misses.

In the third place, protesting is a more complex form of communicative engagement than simply informing and persuading; it also involves changing sensibilities and transforming the political imagination. Protest can not only enrich, but also critically *transform* the public sphere in ontological and epistemic ways: creating publics that did not exist before, creating audiences that did not exist before, and developing forms of understanding, knowledge, and imagination that can be the basis for new social identities and new social relations. For example, abolitionism transformed our social world not simply because the abolitionist movement *informed* and eventually *persuaded* society about the evils of slavery, but more importantly because participants in this protest movement developed new forms of association, new communities with different sensibilities, because they learned and taught others how to change themselves and how to change the world, because they generated new forms of understanding, new visions and conceptions of justice. As the analyses of *The Epistemology of Protest*[6] show, similar things can be said about the women's movement and the LGBTQ + movement, and about the deep transformations of the public sphere that

---

6 Medina *The Epistemology of Protest: Silencing, Epistemic Activism, and the Communicative Life of Protest*, 2023.

these movements accomplished through protest. Let me now turn to key transformations that, on my performative view, protest can accomplish: the creation of protesting publics or communities of resistance, and the prefiguration of new worlds, that is, other-worldly communal practices or alternative world-making.

1. B. PROTEST AS A PERFORMATIVE MECHANISM OF GROUP-CONSTITUTION AND PREFIGURATION.

How can experiences of injustice be turned into a rebellious critical consciousness? How do oppressed subjects become resistant and capable of expressing their resistance in protest acts? How can this be achieved especially when there is a cultivated silence that blocks every attempt to speak up against the injustice in question, when there is no language readily available to denounce the injustice, and when there are all kinds of disincentives and costly consequences to protest? How does a resistant political awareness that can lead people to protest injustice emerge? Although there have been rich discussions of resistance in the recent literature, more needs to be said about the political and communicative-epistemic activities that go into the making of a resistant subjectivity and pave the way to a protesting public mobilizing itself and appearing as such in the public sphere.

My discussions of protest in my most recent book, *The Epistemology of Protest*,[7] elucidate the embryonic forms of protest or proto-protests in which a critical consciousness or sensibility is emerging, and not emerging unimpeded but having to negotiate all kinds of roadblocks and challenges that make it difficult for such new sensibility to emerge in the first place and to express itself. It is for this reason that I pay so much attention to the difficulties of coming to protest when a protest language or critical discourse is lacking and there are strong resistances to the emergence of any such language or critical discourse. It is for this reason that I think it is so important to call attention to subtle and often non-verbal forms of protest (embryonic proto-protests) in which political discomfort and tentative forms of resistance are beginning to emerge.

A central goal of my performative account of protest is to move away from a narrow understanding of protest as requiring prior political organization and appearing in the public sphere fully organized and with a fully developed protesting voice and a fully formed message. As an alternative, my view offers a broader understanding of protest that includes not only spontaneous forms of uprising, but also semi-public and

7 Ibid

tentative ways of expressing political discomfort and reaching out to others to explore whether they could or should resist a given political state of affairs or oppressive situation. I address the roadblocks facing this kind of emerging protesting consciousness and the process of coming to protest by focusing on protest as a performative mechanism for group-constitution or for the formation of communities of resistance. In *The Epistemology of Protest*[8] I explain in detail, focusing on queer activism and anti-racist activism, how resistant subjectivities and critical (or counter-) imaginations, far from pre-existing protest, actually emerge from protest actions and from bonding together in resistance, in particular, through the performative expression of critical emotions not only through words, but also through images and body language. As an example, think of the same-sex kiss-ins and other visibility actions that queer activists engaged in to protest the invisibilization and policing of non-heterosexual people from 1990 on, which I will discuss in some detail in the next section. As this example reveals, the role of affect and emotional expressivity in the complex communication that takes place in and around protest is indeed crucial to understand the kind of critical awakening that goes into the formation

---

8 Ibid

of the critical consciousness of a protesting public and its resistant imagination.

How do victims of injustice undergo a process of *critical awakening* through which they come to experience their situation as an injustice? How do people become motivated to protest and form a community of resistance? As Lisa Guenther rightfully points out, this critical awakening requires an "epistemic shift."[9] Guenther remarks that this shift involves the following: "To understand myself as having something to protest, I must believe that I have been wronged, that I deserve better, and that the situation is open to change."[10] This preliminary description of the epistemic shift involved in the critical awakening of protesters is both too weak and too strong. It is too weak because in order to conceptualize my situation as experiencing an injustice that is worthy of being protested, it is not sufficient that I understand myself as having been wronged and deserving better; it is also required that one develops the capacity (or sensitivity) to understand other subjects experiencing similar situations as having been wronged and deserving better as well. In other words, in order to be able to understand

---

9 Guenther, Lisa "The Emergence and Uptake of Protest" *Contemporary Political Theory* (in press) 2023.

10 Ibid

oneself as having been wronged *as a matter of justice*, one needs to become capable of *connecting* one's situation and experience of being wronged with that of others. This is what Guenther goes on to label, very aptly, *epistemic stretching*, which is indeed a crucial element in the critical awakening of protesters. This epistemic stretching is no small epistemic achievement, and when it does not happen, victims of injustice do not develop a desire to protest, but rather, as Guenther puts it, "a desire to manage their situation from day to day, or to solve the problem at a personal level."[11] As Guenther correctly observes, the critical awakening that can turn victims of injustice into protesters involves not only an "epistemic shift," but also a motivational shift. Victims of injustice need to become motivated to advocate not only for their own sake but also for others, that is, to advocate for justice, for collective (and not just individual) liberation.[12]

On the other hand, Guenther's preliminary formulation of the critical awakening of protesters is a bit too strong if it is taken to require the belief that the situation being protested will change. She goes on to say that victims of injustice may or may not have evidence for that belief.[13] That

11 Ibid

12 Ibid

13 Ibid

is indeed true, but such belief is not required as part of the critical awakening of protesters. A victim who protests injustice may not believe that a world without such injustice is attainable and on the horizon. Confidence that the world will change for the better is not required to protest and engage in practices of resistance. It still makes sense to protest even when one does not think that their situation will change. It makes sense to protest in order to make known to the world, or perhaps just to those who suffer similar harms, that their treatment is unjust. It is in this sense, as I have discussed at length elsewhere (chapter 4 of my 2023), that W.E.B. DuBois emphasized the crucial significance of protest for maintaining one's self- dignity in the face of injustice even when the elimination of the injustice in question is not yet on the political horizon.[14]

Although belief or certainty in the changeability of the world is not required, a defiant imaginative capacity and the capacity to act on that resistant imagination are indeed a crucial part of protest and resistance. As I will explain in detail in the next two sections, communities of resistance are created and sustained around the imaginative capacity to envision that the world can be

---

14 Du Bois, W. E. B. *The Souls of Black Folk* (New York: Penguin Classics, 1903).

otherwise, and around communal practices that reject the world as it is, suspend the norms of the dominant world, and *prefigure* another world. I do endorse a weaker version of Guenther's claim about the need for protesters to experience the world as in principle "open to change" along the lines she suggests later in her commentary of my book, *The Epistemology of Protest*, when she observes that "the desire to engage in protest involves a distinctive interpretation of the world as not yet capable of rendering justice, but still open to the sort of changes that could make it so."[15] Protesting does involve gesturing toward—or *prefiguring*—a more just world, even if the belief in the attainability of such world is not warranted by the present circumstances. Although engaging in protest does not require having already developed an alternative political imaginary, protesting is itself the kind of exercise in political communication that has the potential to develop such alternative political imaginary. In the next two sections I will discuss how the communities of resistance created and sustained by protest can develop a resistant imagination in action that can *prefigure* a more just world.

---

15 Guenther "The Emergence and Uptake of Protest," 2023.

2. COMMUNITIES OF RESISTANCE AND PREFIGURATION: "THE FUTURE IS NOW"

In the late 1970's political theorist Carl Boggs coined the term "prefigurative politics" to refer to the political practices of a group or social movement that demonstrate and embody "those forms of social relations, decision-making, culture, and human experience" that the group or movement aspires to bring about in the world.[16] Prefigurative politics can be described as a politics of disruption that intervenes in the social world to depart from it and suspend its norms, but also as a politics of creation and of community-building. As I conceive it, following Boggs and other neo-Marxist theorists[17] prefigurative politics has three key features. First, it involves a departure from or breakage with the socio-political world and its norms. Second, it involves an other-worldly orientation and the participation in practices of world-making. Third, it also involves the cultivation of social bonds and community attachments invested in alternative world-making, that is, the cultivation

---

16 Boggs, Carl. "Marxism, Prefigurative Communism, and the Problem of Workers' Control," *Radical America* 11 no 6 (November 1977): 100.

17 Monticelli, Lara. *The Future Is Now: An Introduction to Prefigurative Politics (Alternatives to Capitalism in the 21st Century)* (Bristol: Bristol University Press, 2022).

of a community of resistance. This last point about community-building has been highlighted as the central element of prefigurative politics by Wini Breines.[18] Breines emphasizes that prefigurative politics rests on a strong notion of community that involves a network of relations of care that are more personal and intimate than the formal, abstract, and instrumental relations characteristic of contemporary societies. Breines writes: "The crux of prefigurative politics imposed substantial tasks, the central one being to create and sustain within the live practice of the movement, relationships and political forms that 'prefigured' and embodied the desired society."[19] In the forms of sociality that a community of resistance practices, in its everyday social activities, a new social world emerges: a world that is performatively created or *anticipated* in the resistant actions of the community.

This idea of performative creation or *anticipation* of a utopian future in the world-making activities of an alternative community of care is the centerpiece of the powerful idea of "the future in the present" developed by political activist and theorist from Trinidad, C.L.R. James, a key

---

18   Breines, Wini. *Community and Organization in the New Left, 1962-1968: The Great Refusal* (New Brunswick, NJ: Rutgers University Press, 1989), 421.

19   Ibid

contributor to Black Marxist theory in the late twentieth century. In his collection of essays *The Future in the Present*, James argues that socialism is not an utopian future out of reach to present working-class communities, but in fact it is a future that exists in the now, that is, in forms of sociality and relations of care that exist in actual communities of factory workers in the present.[20] [21] According to James, a socialist future can be glimpsed at by observing the egalitarian inter-actions among workers; their egalitarian com-munal practices prefigure and thus anticipate a socialist future. James describes these communi-ties as "outposts of a new society," as an already existing socialist present.[22]

In *Cruising Utopia*, José Muñoz applies James' idea of "the future in the present" to subversive queer practices, arguing that a utopian queer future

20 James, C.L.R. *The Future in the Present: Selected Writings* (New York: L. Hill Books, 1977).

21 James offered the following example: "In one depart-ment of a certain plant in the US there is a worker who is physically incapable of carrying out his duties. But he is a man with wife and children and his condition is due to the strain of previous work in the plant. The workers have organized their work so that for ten years he has had practically nothing to do." 1974; 137

22 James, C.L.R., Lee, Grace C., Chaulieu Pierre and Corne-lius Castoriadis *Facing Reality* (Detroit: Bewick, 1974).

exists in the present when it is performatively produced by queer sexual practices such as cruising.[23] According to Muñoz, these subversive practices transform the spaces in which they occur into "outposts" of a new queer world; these practices perform a radical break or departure from the heteronormative world in such a way that a queer world erupts in the present. Cruising outdoor spaces and gay bathhouses of the 1970's and 1980's (before the AIDS pandemic), Muñoz argues, were "sites of embodied and performed queer politics," "outposts of actually existing queer worlds."[24] Muñoz analyzes cruising sites and gay bath houses of that era as queer utopian places where "normal time" and "normal(ized) living" were suspended, opening up the possibility of the emergence of another time and another way of living, a queer time and a queer form of life. In these subversive sexual practices, Muñoz claims, we find "an ensemble of social actors performing a queer world."[25] "Public sexual culture revealed the existence of a queer world."[26]

---

23 Muñoz, José. *Cruising Utopia: The Then and There of Queer Futurity* (New York: New York University Press, 2009).

24 Ibid 49

25 Ibid

26 Ibid 52

Muñoz's examples of cruising sites and gay bath houses as sites of queer world-making open themselves easily to the two main objections that critics of prefigurative politics raise: *naiveté* and *escapism*. In the first place, the objection of naiveté proceeds by ascribing to those who engage in prefigurative politics cognitively misguided attitudes, false beliefs, or misplaced certainty: "just because they momentarily interrupt the world as we know it, because they create a diversion or disruption, they *believe* they can bring about a new world."[27] Yet, this objection misunderstands what prefigurative protest actions are: they are not about predicting the future and they do not require any particular kind of belief about the future. As argued in the previous section, belief or certainty in upcoming social change is not required for protesting current conditions and performatively gesturing toward alternative social realities.

Along similar lines, the Marxist thesis that proletariat communities and their forms of life "anticipate" a coming sociality has come under attack in contemporary critical theory. Daniel Loick, for example, argues that we should reject the Marxist thesis of *anticipation* because it is predicated on a problematic philosophy of history according to which an upcoming

---

27 Ibid

revolution is dialectically inevitable.[28] As an alternative to this philosophy-of-history thesis, Loick proposes what he calls an "anthropological thesis" as the proper way to understand the Marxist view of the superiority of the proletariat and of other oppressed communities. It is not that these communities have a *cognitive* superiority because they embody the "truths" of the future, but rather, they have an *ethical* superiority because they can show us how to live an egalitarian human life. As Loick puts it, the *ethical* superiority of oppressed communities resides in the fact that they "have an already-present access to specific social potentials," not in the fact that their "way of existence *anticipates* a coming sociality."[29] As Loick puts it, the living "truth" that the practices of oppressed communities embody is that "'humanness' cannot be realized inside this existing society [...]. the only opportunity to stay 'human' in 'inhuman surroundings' is through another form of community: *a counter-community*."[30] Loick writes:

---

28 Loick, Daniel. "The Ethical Life of Counter-Communities" *Critical Times* 4 no 1 (April 2021) 1-28. DOI 10.1215/26410478-8855203.

29 Ibid 1

30 Ibid 15

> It is precisely those communities whose
> everyday life is marked by experiences of
> suffering and misery that develop an access
> to epistemic insights, moral attitudes, and
> aesthetic expressions that privileged subjects
> lack. Throughout history, countless groups of
> excluded and exploited people have insisted
> that their form of life is in a certain sense
> superior to the one of their oppressors.[31]

According to Loick, the *anticipation* thesis
requires a confidence in a better future that cannot be had after "the shattering of the certainty of
a pending communist revolution;"[32] and it leaves
the oppressed subject "empty-handed in the present: she can do nothing more than wait until his-
torical reality catches up to her already cultivated
way of existence."[33] By contrast, Loick rightly
emphasizes that the anthropological understanding of the superiority of the oppressed subject
who rebels against domination avoids these prob-
lems. It does not require a misplaced confidence
in the future, nor does it leave the oppressed subject empty-handed in the present, since oppressed
communities that develop alternative and more

---

31 Ibid 2

32 Ibid 5

33 Ibid 7

humane ways of living find *realization* and *satisfaction* in the present, in their *counter*-practices or "counter-collectivization." Loick argues that *counter-communities* (that is, communities created "by a certain *distancing* from dominant social structures, a *counter*-movement") contain positive experiences of enjoyment and a positive affective life that "stems directly from the vital collective experience of being-against"[34], "feelings of satisfaction or even euphoria," a "paradoxical feeling of joy amid sorrow"; "an experience of consolation, joy, or even a certain recalcitrant form of happiness, which finds its base precisely in not being integrated into the hegemonic society."[35] These enjoyments and positive affective experiences ("satisfaction," "ecstasy," etc.) that Loick discusses are not simply a result of an "expectation of a coming redemption," but the result of experiencing and enjoying a kind of sociality or communal practices that is here and now, enacted and enjoyed by the resistors in the community of resistance as it exists. This positive affective life is not future-dependent or predicated on a future-expectation: the resistors experience it because they are enacting a new form of sociality, performatively demonstrating and experiencing it in the here and now, whatever their beliefs and

---

34 Ibid 5

35 Ibid 2

expectations about whether or not that form of sociality or communal practice will catch on and will become something available to all outside the margins, whether or not it will migrate from sub-cultures/counter-cultures to mainstream culture. As Loick reminds us, Marx insisted that "noninte-gration into bourgeois society by itself provides the excluded with other sources of vitality and happi-ness."[36] Finding out in practice that another life is possible, that there is an alternative social space and community outside the oppressive system one is under, is the source of positive emotions and attach-ments, feelings of hope, love, and appreciation, that can be found in communities of resistance.

I fully agree with Loick's general theory of the ethical life of counter-communities and the important points he makes about counter-collec-tivization. Yet, I think that he is too quick in giv-ing up on the idea that counter-practices *anticipate* liberatory futures, especially if we understand this idea in a performative (rather than predictive) way and through C.L.R. James' notion of "the future in the present." It is certainly true that, when understood in a narrowly cognitive and predictive sense, the thesis of anticipation is untenable. Still, the claim that communities of resistance *antici-pate* new forms of sociality can (and should!) be

---

36 Ibid 13

understood as the claim that their counter-practices performatively (not predictively) *prefigure* alternative futures. Loick is certainly right that "the actual life of the oppressed does not draw its superiority from anticipating a future liberation."[37] This is true, but there is something *anticipatory* in the practices of counter-communities nonetheless, the glimpse of a possible future in the actual present; there is something *prefigurative* there. When properly understood as performative prefiguration or enactment of the future, rather than as prediction, the idea of anticipation of alternative worlds and alternative futures is in fact fully compatible with Loick's anthropological view of the actual access and enjoyment of social potentialities of counter-communities. In fact, thus understood, the anticipatory (or prefigurative) and the anthropological are not only compatible, but in fact mutually supporting interpretations of communities of resistance, which jointly underscore the dual meaning of "counter-collectivization."

Loick applies his general theory of the ethical life of counter-communities to queer and diasporic forms of collectivity. So, following Loick's account, it is not difficult to see how queer sexual practices, such as the ones analyzed by

---

37 Ibid 14

Muñoz, are immune to the objection of naiveté: they certainly don't require misplaced predictive certainty or a false confidence in the future; they are about the social potentialities realized and enjoyed in the present. However, there is a second objection that seems to have force against Muñoz's account of queer futurity in sexual counter-cultural practices: *escapism*. What if these practices, instead of being a form of radical world-making, were nothing but a form of world-*escaping*? What if the joys and pleasures of queer counter-cultural practices were simply selfish and apolitical, a form of evasion? What if those subversive moments that happen in the interstices of the social world do not amount to a form of sociality (a counter-community and its counter-collectivization) that can transform the world and lead to the construction of a different world? In other words, the worry here is that counter-practices may only provide a false sense of liberation and become a way of escaping, an evasion or diversion that postpones the revolution, a way of taking time off from revolutionary struggles in order to have some fun, partying on the side instead of fighting to change the world, so to speak. The worry of escapism does not apply when there is a deep commitment to transforming the world, rather than simply escaping it momentarily, when there are sustained efforts at organizing, fighting for transformative justice, and constructing an alternative world.

Yet, is this true of cruising and queer sexual practices in gay bath houses? Do we have a non-escapist prefigurative politics there?

While it is not difficult to image that there are escapist elements to some subversive queer practices such as cruising or gay-bathhouse activities, this certainly does not apply to all subversive queer practices that we can find in the history of queer politics and activism. In fact, Muñoz's examples of cruising sites and gay bathhouses don't seem to be the best examples of subversive queer practices for prefigurative politics. The worry of escapism does apply to sporadic subversive practices, such as cruising or non-normative sexual activities at a bathhouse, which can bring temporary relief while being detached (or at least detachable) from organized communities of resistance devoted to transforming the world. This is why, in my view, escapism is a legitimate worry for the queer practices that Munoz focuses on. These subversive sexual practices do not seem to be tied to queer organizing and queer communities of resistance. I agree with Muñoz that in the cruising activities and gay bathhouse sexual practices of the late twentieth century we can see a critical subversive potential. Indeed, we can see there the suspension of heteronormative space and time,

the cultivation of other-worldly orientations and
the performative enactment of a queer world.
However, were those who participated in these
practices members of a *community of resistance*?
Does a cruising network or a gay bathhouse cli-
entele (which often include closeted and con-
servative subjects) amount to a *community of
resistance* or *counter-community*? It is not clear
that we can see in those heterogenous groups a
political community of resistance, that is, a community committed to subversive politics and the
deep transformation of the mainstream world—
in fact, many people who frequented gay bathhouses and cruising sites have been known to be
simply taking a break from the heteronormative
world only to return to it as active participants
(among them were Republican politicians who
supported homophobic policies). Yet, there are
plenty of examples in queer activism of communities of resistance committed to subversive politics and the performative enactment of a queer
world. A prime example of a queer community
of resistance engaged in prefigurative politics
is Queer Nation. Let me conclude this section
with a brief analysis of the non-escapist and
transformative prefigurative politics that the
protest actions of Queer Nation exemplify.

Queer Nation was founded in the Spring of
1990 in New York City, and very quickly Queer

Nation chapters were established in many major US cities. Queer Nation was created as a non-hierarchical and decentralized grassroots organization to protest and resist the escalation of violence against queer people and the rampant homophobic and transphobic biases in the media, sports, the arts, and in most aspects of public life. Queer Nation became well known very quickly for its confrontational tactics, its provocative slogans, and its visibility protest actions such as kiss-ins. The inaugural protest act of Queer Nation was a kiss-in that was staged as a visibility action at Flutie's, a New York straight bar, on April 13, 1990. That night, dozens of same-sex couples entered Flutie's and started making out, deeply disrupting the heteronormative expectations that had structured that space up to that point, to the discomfort of (at least some of) the establishment's regular clients. Visibility protest actions of this sort sponsored by Queer Nation came to be known as "Queer Nights Out" and became popular in some metropolitan areas in the 1990's.[38]As I

---

38 Probably the most disruptive and best publicized kiss-in of this kind was organized by Queer Nation/L.A. in 1991 to interrupt the 64th Academy Awards by obstructing entry to the event with a multitude of same-sex couples kissing on the red carpet.

have discussed in detail elsewhere (in chapter 6 of my 2023 book), by storming into a club to "queer" it or by blocking intersections with dozens of same-sex couples kissing, Queer Nation activists did two things simultaneously. In the first place, they forcefully denounced heteronormative and homophobic spaces and unveiled the exclusionary and oppressive norms underlying and structuring those spaces. In the second place, they transformed those spaces with their protest actions so that the spaces themselves, if only momentarily during their performative intervention, became queer spaces in which same-sex couples could safely kiss in public. It is in this way that with their direct actions of queer resistance such as "Queer Nights Out" queer nationals engaged in queer world-making, prefiguring a world without homophobia. Of course, these queer protesters could not be accused of navieté or false confidence in the future: they certainly did not think that their act of resistance had magically abolished homophobia and turned those spaces into queer spaces for good. They knew all too well that the following day queer subjects would experience violence in those very spaces if they dared to express queer affectivity without the support and protection of their community. Nonetheless with their performative interventions queer nationals offered us a glimpse of a queer world. They prefigured a world in which queer sociality could express itself proudly and safely in public, and they did that with an other-worldly orientation that was aiming at transforming the world, rather than simply escaping it. Queer nationals could not be accused of escapism: their goal was not simply to leave the mainstream world as it is while playing at its margins, just for the sake of having some transient fun. It was deeply transformative to be able to experience the joy of safe same-sex kissing in public. It wasn't just pure evasion or a simple momentary moment of pleasure that left no mark in the world.

The anti-assimilationist attitude of Queer Nation was directly connected to its transformative potential and ambitions at world-making. Instead of seeking to make the queer public respectable and assimilated to mainstream culture, Queer Nation encouraged the queer public to feel unapologetic and proud of their sexual lifestyles and of their alternative   communities and countercultures. Queer Nation's protest acts were aimed at affirming the dignity of queer people through the expression of pride in sexual difference, community- building, and self-empowerment. Far from being interested in pleasing mainstream sensibilities, Queer

Nation activists were keen on antagonizing them,
shocking them, and creating all kinds of trouble
for them. For example, they tried to make it as difficult as possible for mainstream publics to ignore
alternative sexualities and look the other way as if
alternative sexualities were something shameful
that could only happen when nobody was looking.
Queer Nation used "in- your-face" slogans and protest tactics that expressed pride in nonconforming
sexual lifestyles and practices.[39] They thought that
the homophobia and erotophobia of a repressive,
puritanical society should be confronted head-on,
and they fought it with unapologetic and aggres-
sive protest tactics, aiming at precipitating urgently
needed social changes. The very name of the organization, *Queer Nation*, modeled after *Black Nation*,
conveyed the constitution of a durable community
of resistance for the transformation of the world:
they were not about finding a place in the social
world as it existed, but rather, about engaging in
radical social transformation and in the construction of a different world: a Queer Nation.

   In my view, the activism of Queer Nation is
exemplary of the kind of prefigurative politics

---

39 For example, they used heavily sexual bumper stickers—
    such as "Proud Cock Sucking Faggot," created by Queer
    Nation/San Francisco in 1990—to aggressively fight
    against stigmatization and promote pride in alternative
    sexualities.

engaged in transformative world-making without falling into navieté or escapism. This kind of queer activism fits well Adrian Kreutz's description of prefigurative politics as:

> "a way of engaging in social change activism that seeks to bring about this other world by means of planting the seeds of the society of the future in the soil of today's. [...] Prefigurativism is a way of showing what a world without the tyranny of the present might look like. It is a way of finding hope (but not escapism!) in the realms of possibility."[40]

Let's look more closely at how the *counter* (or other-worldly) communal practices of prefigurative politics work. How does a community of resistance engage in prefiguration and radical world-making? In the next and final section, drawing from the work of Women of Color feminist scholars Asha Bhandary[41] and

40 Kreutz, Adrian. *Review of Paul Raekstad and Sofa Saio Gradin: Prefigurative Politics: Building Tomorrow Today* (Cambridge, Polity Press, 2020); https://marxandphilosophy.org.uk/reviews/17886_prefigurative-politics-building-tomorrow-today-by-paul-raekstad-and-sofa-saio-gradin-reviewed-by-adrian-kreutz/.

41 Bhandary "Caring for Whom? Racial Practices of Care and Liberal Constructivism," 2020.

Saidiya Hartman,[42] I will elucidate how the protest actions of counter-communities leave traces of resistance and subversion in the world, tracks for other resistors to follow, prefiguring alternative worlds and futures.

3. RESISTANT IMAGINATIONS IN ACTION: *LIVING COUNTERFACTUALLY* AND EMPOWERMENT THROUGH COUNTER-COMMUNAL PRACTICES OF RESISTANCE

In my view, counter-communal practices of resistance are the performative exercise of the counter-imagination. They are, literally, resistant imaginations *in action*. How do subjects and communities do that, and what is the normative force and transformative potential of those performative expressions of the resistant imagination? In this final section, I will try to answer these questions through an examination of two crucial dimensions of counter communal practices (or what Loick calls "counter-collectivization"): their *oppositional* dimension and their *experimentalist* or *creative* dimension.

---

42 Hartman *Wayward Lives, Beautiful Experiments: Intimate Histories of Riotous Black Girls, Troublesome Women, and Queer Radicals*, 2019.

In the first place, communities of resistance have an *oppositional* dimension which they exercise by resisting injustice and imagining a world in which we could live more justly. This is what political theorist Jane Mansbridge has described as the "oppositional consciousness" that emerges from liberation movements.[43] As Mansbridge emphasizes, liberation movements are formed around members of an oppressed group who do not have standing and/or cannot find a voice in the discursive spaces available; so that they have to mobilize to develop a *new voice* and exercise their expressive agency in ways that carve out *new communicative spaces and dynamics.* As Mansbridge puts it, they "need to create autonomous spaces."[44] This can be exemplified by the way in which the queer liberation movement created spaces for people to denounce homophobic and transphobic oppression and to think and communicate about their sexual and gender identity and their rights and freedoms, outside the constraints of the institutions and

---

43 Mansbridge, Jane. "The Making of Oppositional Consciousness," (eds.) Jane Mansbridge and Aldon Morris, *Oppositional Consciousness: The Subjective Roots of Social Protest* (Chicago: University of Chicago Press, 2001) 1-19.

44 Ibid 8

dominant ideology of heteronormativity and gender normativity. Think especially of the early LGBTQ+ protests against police harassment: the first trans uprising in May 1959 at the 24-hour Cooper Do-nuts cafe in Los Angeles, which came to be known as "the Cooper Do-nuts Riot"; and the iconic, spontaneous demonstrations by members of the LGBTQ+ community in response to a police raid in New York City on Jun 28, 1969, which came to be known as "the Stonewall Riots." Think also of the disruptive kiss-ins of Queer Nation examined in the previous section. These communal actions of resistance have the potential to produce *normative* and *ontological* transformations in the social world. Resistors express their oppositional consciousness in their actions by speaking and acting differently, and creating new spaces of interaction in which unjust norms are denounced, suspended and replaced; spaces structured by different normative orientations. This is how resistors engage in liberatory ways of world-making, exercising their resistant imagination in action in a way that carves out a new space in the world, changing the world and giving us a glimpse of a different world.

The oppositional normative orientation embodied in action just described fits well what Asha Bhandary has called "living counterfactually."

She writes: "*Living counterfactually*, as a minority woman, means asserting full claimant status in micro-interactions in the workplace, in one's community, and generally, in both private and impersonal spaces."[45] Living counterfactually means living "as if the world were otherwise," "as if affordances are present when they do not exist."[46] It involves the exercise of the resistant imagination. It starts with *counter-imagining* or imagining the world otherwise, in opposition to unjust present conditions; and it continues by acting and living according to that counter-imagination. For example, this is one possible starting point of the counter-imagination for living counterfactually, as suggested by Bhandary: "Imagine a world in which people of color refuse to care for white people."[47]

Bhandary goes on to explain that when women of color live counterfactually according to this counter-imagination, it will reveal how the unfair normative expectations of white privilege operate: for example, in the workplace, it will reveal "the mammification of women of color in white collar workplaces," and how "minority women who

---

45 Bhandary "Caring for Whom? Racial Practices of Care and Liberal Constructivism," 3.

46 Ibid

47 Ibid

are not caring and deferential are quickly labeled 'uncollegial.'"[48]

Because living counterfactually involves violating the normative expectations of white privilege, it will bring about negative reactions and repercussions, painfully revealing the costs of living otherwise. Bhandary emphasizes the *diagnostic* significance of living counterfactually: it helps us to identify the normative failures of the actual world, the distance needed to be traveled from the unjust world we live in to a more just world. This is how Bhandary describes the diagnostic power of living counterfactually in revealing how privilege works and how it has to be dismantled:

> Because Latinas, Black, Indigenous, Arab, Asian, and/or Brown Women are expected to attend and defer to others, asserting full claimant status from this social position *reveals* the challenges and the requirements of the radical social change required to achieve justice. To move through the world as a woman of color asserting full claimant status is like sending iodine contrast into an artery prior to a CT scan. It supplies contrast through which to diagnose the system. And, like this injection, it can burn."[49]

---

48 Ibid
49 Ibid

When oppressed subjects engage in living counterfactually, unfair normative expectations and privileges are revealed by the negative reactions expressed by the holders of those expectations and privileges, "the subjectivities that supervene on the unjust caregiving arrangement become evident through their holders' expressions of rogue emotions, violence in its many forms, microaggressions, and confusion."[50] As Bhandary puts it, when women of color refuse to provide the care and deference unfairly expected from them, "social inequalities and sedimented hierarchies are revealed," often "through overt violence as well as microaggressions which together betray 'liberal' societies' caregiving substructures."[51] But note that living counterfactually can be more than a diagnostic tool; it can also be a *prefigurative* tool: a tool for the anticipation of a more just world, a mechanism of world-making, especially when done in concert with others, as a cultivated practice of resistance of a counter-community.

Bhandary stops short of assigning socio-ontological significance to *living counterfactually* because those who live counterfactually do not receive proper uptake by others and therefore do not succeed in producing a shared and socially

---

50 Ibid

51 Ibid

accepted world. Living counterfactually is living "in ways that are not permitted, and also in ways that *do not exist in a robust ontological sense* based on the social meanings of our actions. We are living as if we are in *a possible world, one that does not currently exist.*"[52] Note that although the world that the resistors engaged in living counterfactually try to produce is not shared by all, and especially not by those who are protective of the unfair privileges being dismantled, this possible world is nonetheless shared by those who are resisting together, by those who live counterfactually and by like-minded social actors. So, while in one sense, the possible world performed by resistors living counterfactually is not the actual world— that is, it is not the dominant world we all live in—in another, very important sense, that possible world *becomes an actual world* in and through the resistant actions of those living counterfactually: it is partially produced, made present, performatively enacted. Those who live counterfactually performatively *actualize* a possible world, making it exist at least partially in the here and now.

Talking about the resistant actions of women of color, Bhandary says that "the completion of a woman of color's expression of agency does not occur" because "our expressions of full

---

52 Ibid 4

claimant status do not receive the proper uptake," and "although we put forth an action, the meaning we enact is not the meaning it gains from dominantly positioned interlocutors, and therefore the action is not completed."[53] But although the action is not completed and cannot have the full performative effects in the world that would have if it were to receive proper uptake, the resistant action does occur and it leaves a mark in the world, especially in the social world of those living counterfactually, who can see their counter-imagination expressed and find a place in the world for it. We could say with Bhandary that the resistant actions of those who live counterfactually is not completed, but they are underway; and therefore, these actions are *prefigurative*: their world-making may not be completed, but it is underway; they prefigure another world. Living counterfactually involves the cultivation of a disregard with respect to present conditions and the cultivation of an orientation with respect to alternative futures, which open up new possibilities of world-making. The disregard for the present and the orientation toward a future world yet to come are precisely the key elements of the *hos me* or "as if not" attitude characteristic of early Christian communities that

---

53 Ibid 4

Giorgio Agamben describes as engaged in revolutionary forms of living.[54]

Living counterfactually is not just a thought experiment, but an *experiment of living*, to use Saidiya Hartman's phrase. What Saidiya Hartman describes as the "beautiful experiments of living" of "riotous black girls" and "queer radicals" in New York and Philadelphia at the beginning of the twentieth century are perfect examples of counterfactual living that creates counter-worlds.[55] Hartman describes in detail the new forms of intimate relations and community living developed by young urban black women living in poverty and under oppressive forms of surveillance that criminalized them and pathologized them. Hartman examines these "beautiful experiments of living" not only as ways of surviving and escaping criminalization and pathologization, but also as inventive ways of thriving and creating insurgent counter-cultures. This brings us to the second crucial feature of counter-communal practices of resistance: namely, their *creative* power or *inventiveness*. The communities of "riotous black girls" and "queer radicals" of the early

---

54 Agamben, Giorgio. *The Time That Remains: A Commentary on the Letter to the Romans* (Stanford, CA: Stanford University Press, 2005).

55 Hartman *Wayward Lives, Beautiful Experiments: Intimate Histories of Riotous Black Girls, Troublesome Women, and Queer Radicals*, 2019.

twentieth century that Hartman studies refused to live the lives that had been scripted for them: as respectable monogamous partners in heteronormative relations, as respectable domestic and service workers, as respectable second-class citizens; and they engaged in an "intimate revolution" through which they *created* alternative ways of life and alternative social worlds. According to Hartman, in these communities we find "a *beautiful experiment* in how-to-live."[56] She calls the lives of the members of these communities of resistance *wayward lives* because waywardness is "the practice of the social otherwise, the insurgent ground that enables new possibilities and new vocabularies"[57]; "waywardness is a practice of possibility at a time when all roads, except the ones created by *smashing out*, are foreclosed."[58] [59] The new forms of sociality and alternative forms of living developed by oppressed communities created new social worlds in the interstices of the dominant

---

56 Ibid 228

57 Ibid 227-228

58 Ibid 228

59 Hartman emphasizes that "wayward" is "related to the family of words: errant, fugitive, recalcitrant, anarchic, willful, reckless, troublesome, riotous, tumultuous, rebellious and wild"; and that it means "to wander, to be unmoored, adrift, rambling, roving, cruising, strolling, and seeking." 227, 2019.

world. The very lives of the members of these communities constituted a form of embodied, performative resistance: they lived counterfactually, whether they did so self-consciously and as a result of a political awakening or not; and their living otherwise became constitutive of another world, a counter-cultural world. Interestingly enough, there seems to be something in common in the subversive counter-communal practices of the "riotous black girls" and "queer radicals" of the early twentieth century that Hartman describes and the counter-communal practices of the early Christian communities that Giorgio Agamben (2005) describes: their disregard for the dominant conditions of the present and their other-worldly orientation endow their communal agency with transcendent creativity and their "beautiful experiments of living" with world-transforming power.

The two features of counter-communal practices that I have highlighted, their oppositional and creative aspects, are of course internally related: these counter-practices of resistance interrupt the world as we know it in order to create another world. These two aspects are brought together in Daniel Loick's account of "counter-collectivization," that is, of the processes of community formation that go into the making of counter-communities. The making of an alternative community in this robust sense involves the development of an alternative normative economy or alternative ethical life that does not depend on the norms and forms of recognition and respect of the dominant, mainstream world. As Loick puts it, this is "a possibility that Hegel opens up but never fully explores: the possibility that servants, instead of seeking recognition from their masters, start recognizing each other."[60] "Recognition among servants knits together an underground, subcutaneous normative web that stands in permanent conflict with the established world—an antagonistic counter-ethical life."[61] Marx, neo- Marxist philosophers and recent critical theorists have explored this possibility. Charles Taylor and Axel Honneth, for example, have argued for a politics of collective self-affirmation through the independent recognition of oppressed subjects among themselves. Honneth describes the alternative normative economies of recognition developed by disenfranchised groups as "countercultures of respect"; and he argues that the alternative forms of recognition developed by these countercultures are *compensatory*: they compensate for the recognition deficits accrued by subjects who have been oppressed or marginalized.[62] In his

---

60 Loick "The Ethical Life of Counter-Communities," 7.

61 Ibid

62 Honneth, Axel. *The I in We: Studies in the Theory of Recognition* (London: Polity, 2012).

critical engagement with Honneth, Loick argues that counter-communities are not merely compensatory, but *transcendent*.

What Loick calls the transcendent aspect of counter-communities involves precisely the two features I have emphasized in this section: the opposition against and interruption of the dominant world, or, as Loick puts it, echoing Marx, the *abolition* of the present conditions; and the creation of new worlds and social orders.[63]

Loick argues that Honneth's account misses "the specific ethical potential of counter- communities" by construing the recognition processes of these communities as imitative of and parasitic on the norms of dominant society, without fully acknowledging "the transgressive elements of the ethical life of the subjugated." "The ethical life of counter-communities is neither compensatory nor deficient, but antagonistic and thus *transcendent*. It demands not integration to the existing order but its *abolition*."[64] Loick rightly emphasizes that "it is precisely the rupture of everyday life that opens up the possibility of a better society," or the creation of an alternative world.[65] Following Marx, Loick uses as an example the abolition of the patriarchal and

---

63 Loick "The Ethical Life of Counter-Communities".

64 Ibid 4

65 Ibid 2

heteronormative bourgeois notion of the family and the creation of new forms of sociality in the queer and feminist movement. Marx thought that it was the alternative forms of living of economically oppressed communities that would abolish the bourgeois notion of the family, but as Loick argues, "it is not so much the proletariat but queer and feminist movements that pose a fundamental challenge to the traditional family form, contesting the exclusivity and the conformism of conventional models of kinship."[66] Instead of seeking integration in and equal access to the established normative order, many queer and feminist subcultures, "seek to develop new forms of collectivity that fundamentally contest hegemonic models of intimacy and generativity—they are not compensatory but transcendent. Such critiques are rooted in the ethical life of counter-communities, encompassing radically oppositional body practices, desires, economies, networks, and, as Jack Halberstam says, other 'willfully eccentric modes of being.'"[67] Loick also sees the transcendent aspects of abolitionist and liberatory processes of counter-collectivization highlighted in Lauren Berlant and Michael Warner's account of queer subcultures as radical "world-making," as involving "world-making

---

66 Ibid 16

67 Ibid

projects [that] are marked by an irreducible open-
ness and a becoming" and depart "from all forms
of familial or national identity formation."[68] Loick
emphasizes that this is just one of the many abolitionist and revolutionary struggles in which counter-
communities are engaged in order to transform the
world. While Marx believed that there was a single
and unified revolutionary class that could provide
an alternative ethical life and a path to a different
future without domination, Loick emphasizes that
there are plural and piecemeal processes of counter-collectivization that abolish present conditions
and gesture toward— *prefigure*, I would say—liberatory futures in the present.

There are indeed multiple and heterogeneous
communities of resistance that struggle to change
the world in multiple fronts and engage in different
forms of alternative world-making. This plurality
and heterogeneity within and across communities
of resistance complicate struggles for liberation
while also providing multiple sites for exerting both
out-group and in- group friction that can be used as
opportunities for growth and for expanding political horizons and sensibilities. As Loick puts it, each

> counter-community exists within the broader
> ethical life of dominant society and within

---

68 See Berlant, Lauren, and Michael Warner "Sex in Pub-
    lic." *Critical Inquiry* 24 no. 2 (Winter 1998): 547–66.

or alongside other (counter-)communities that also might be in different stages in their respective collectivization processes. The multiplication of non- simultaneous, heterogeneous ethical lives produces irreducible *friction and conflict*. I can participate in multiple ethical lives at once, generating collisions of normative expectations and claims; furthermore, a community can in one respect be dominated and dominant in another, especially in a global context.[69]

Liberatory struggles are full of friction and conflict. The friction among alternative sensibilities and imaginations is what I have called *epistemic resistance*[70] which is something that is cultivated in a concerted and sustained way within movements of liberation. As I have analyzed in *The Epistemology of Protest*, liberation movements engage in *epistemic activism*, which consists in organized ways of deploying epistemic friction to meliorate sensibilities and imaginations for egalitarian and liberatory purposes.[71] Epistemic activism creates

---

69 Ibid 18-19

70 Medina, José. *The Epistemology of Resistance: Gender and Racial Oppression, Epistemic Injustice, and Resistant Imaginations* (New York: Oxford University Press, 2013).

71 Medina *The Epistemology of Protest: Silencing, Epistemic Activism, and the Communicative Life of Protest*, 2023.

beneficial epistemic friction (or "good trouble," to use John Lewis' famous phrase) across groups and within groups. The epistemic friction that liberation movements deploy is sometimes outward directed: this is the oppositional dimension of the resistant imagination in action that we can see in counter-communities and their prefigurative political actions. Yet the epistemic friction of liberation movements is also at times inward directed, operating within the communities of resistance, and also within the resistant subjectivities of their members: this is a crucial part of the constructive (or regenerative) dimension of the resistant imagination in action. A key dimension of the imagination in action and of epistemic activism is the regeneration of sensibilities, the constitution of new form of subjectivities and communities. When the resistant imagination becomes embodied in actions, it is a catalyst for transformation not only of the world but of ourselves. In other words, the resistant imagination in action becomes a mechanism of *self-transformation*, a path for the formation of resistant communities and subjectivities. This is an important point of convergence between Loick's neo-Marxist account of counter- collectivization and my prefigurative politics. Loick also points out that the processes of world-transformation that are part of counter-collectivization are at the same time processes of self- transformation. He emphasizes that communities of resistance are formed through "a critical desubjectivation (in the sense of a desubjugation) and […] a radical transformation of the self."[72] And processes of counter-collectivization are not only about *undoing* oppressive forms of subjectivity and community, but also about *creating* new ones and empowering them.

Loick describes beautifully how counter-collectivization involves processes of subject formation and of community formation that are *empowering* sources of agency:

> The formation of a counter-community implies a constant working through of one's own affective constitution. Political practice, then, is never only a struggle against an external adversary, but also a transformation of one's form of life, involving a change of everyday culture and ordinary practice, psychic and physical traits, attention and habits. Audre Lorde has described the affective dimension of this self-transformation as 'metabolism,' enabling oppressed or marginalized subjects to digest society's hate and rejection and convert them into feelings of *empowerment and dignity*."[73] (My emphasis)

---

72 Loick "The Ethical Life of Counter-Communities," 17.

73 Ibid 19

Acting together in resistant ways is self-transformative and epistemically empowering. It is through resistant imaginations in action, thought the counter-practices of liberatory movements prefiguring an alternative world ("a counter-world within the world," as Loick puts it), that new voices and perspectives are empowered and become visible, audible, and efficacious. This kind of epistemic self-empowerment takes place through the subversive, collective actions of communities of resistance, such as the kiss-ins and Queer Nights Out of Queer Nation. Through actions of this sort resistant imaginations become alive, embodied, and efficacious: they create a disruption or interruption in the dominant world and make space for alternative worlds; and thus they performatively prefigure the possibility of a more just world. As I have argued elsewhere,[74] members of democratic societies committed to the freedom and equality of all have a prima facie obligation to participate in (or at least support) the liberatory struggles of communities of resistance, to follow the paths of resistance prefigured by the defiant lives and rebellious acts of those who refuse to accept the world as we find it.

---

74 Medina *The Epistemology of Protest: Silencing, Epistemic Activism, and the Communicative Life of Protest*, 2023.

REFERENCES

Agamben, Giorgio. *The Time That Remains: A Commentary on the Letter to the Romans.* Stanford CA: Stanford University Press, 2005.

Berlant, Lauren, and Michael Warner "Sex in Public." *Critical Inquiry* 24, no. 2 (Winter 1998): 547–66.

Bhandary, Asha Leena. "Caring for Whom? Racial Practices of Care and Liberal Constructivism" *Philosophies* 7, no. 78 (July 2022): 1-14. https://doi.org/10.3390/philosophies7040078.

Boggs, Carl. "Marxism, Prefigurative Communism, and the Problem of Workers' Control."

Radical America 11 no. 6 (November 1977): 99-122.

Breines, Wini. *Community and Organization in the New Left, 1962-1968: The Great Refusal.* New Brunswick, NJ: Rutgers University Press, 1989.

Butler, Judith. *Notes toward a Performative Theory of Assembly.* Cambridge MA: Harvard University Press, 2015.

Cherry, Myisha. "Value-Based Protest Slogans: An Argument for Reorientation" in *The Movement for Black Lives: Philosophical Perspectives*, edited by, Brandon Hogan, Michael Cholbi, Alex Madva, and Benjamin S. Yostr, 160-175, New York: Oxford University Press, 2021.

Du Bois, W. E. B. *The Souls of Black Folk.* New York: Penguin Classics, 1903.

Guenther, Lisa. "The Emergence and Uptake of Protest." *Contemporary Political Theory* (Forthcoming) 2023.

Hartman, Saidiya. *Wayward Lives, Beautiful Experiments: Intimate Histories of Riotous Black Girls, Troublesome Women, and Queer Radicals*. New York: Norton, 2019.

Honneth, Axel. *The I in We: Studies in the Theory of Recognition*. London: Polity, 2012.

James, C.L.R. *The Future in the Present: Selected Writings*. New York: L. Hill Books, 1977.

James, C.L.R. Lee, Grace C., Chaulieu Pierre and Cornelius Castoriadis *Facing Reality*. Detroit MI: Bewick, 1974.

Kreutz, Adrian. "Review of Paul Raekstad and Sofa Saio Gradin: *Prefigurative Politics: Building Tomorrow Today*." Cambridge MA: Polity Press 2020. https://marxandphilosophy.org.uk/reviews/17886_prefigurative-politics-building-tomorrow-today-by-paul-raekstad-and-sofa-saio-gradin-reviewed-by-adrian-kreutz/

Loick, Daniel. "The Ethical Life of Counter-Communities." *Critical Times* 4 no. 1 (April 2021): 1-28. DOI 10.1215/26410478-8855203.

Mansbridge, Jane. "The Making of Oppositional Consciousness," in *Oppositional Consciousness: The Subjective Roots of Social Protest*, edited by Jane Mansbridge and Aldon Morris,Chicago IL: University of Chicago Press, 2001, 1-19.

Medina, José. *The Epistemology of Protest: Silencing, Epistemic Activism, and the Communicative Life of Protest.* New York: Oxford University Press, 2023.

Medina, José. *The Epistemology of Resistance: Gender and Racial Oppression, Epistemic Injustice, and Resistant Imaginations.* New York: Oxford University Press, 2013.

Monticelli, Lara. *The Future Is Now: An Introduction to Prefigurative Politics (Alternatives to Capitalism in the 21st Century)* Bristol: Bristol University Press, 2022.

Muñoz, José. *Cruising Utopia: The Then and There of Queer Futurity.* New York: New York University Press, 2009.

THE AQUINAS LECTURES
Published by the Marquette University Press
Milwaukee WI 53201-1881 USA
http://www.mu.edu/mupress/

1. *St. Thomas and the Life of Learning.* John F. McCormick, S.J. (1937) ISBN 0-87462-101-1
2. *St. Thomas and the Gentiles.* Mortimer J. Adler (1938) ISBN 0-87462-102-X
3. *St. Thomas and the Greeks.* Anton C. Pegis (1939) ISBN 0-87462-103-8
4. *The Nature and Functions of Authority.* Yves Simon (1940) ISBN 0-87462-104-6
5. *St. Thomas and Analogy.* Gerald B. Phelan (1941) ISBN 0-87462-105-4
6. *St. Thomas and the Problem of Evil.* Jacques Maritain (1942) ISBN 0-87462-106-2
7. *Humanism and Theology.* Werner Jaeger (1943) ISBN 0-87462-107-0
8. *The Nature and Origins of Scientism.* John Wellmuth (1944) ISBN 0-87462-108-9
9. *Cicero in the Courtroom of St. Thomas Aquinas.* E.K. Rand (1945) ISBN 0-87462-109-7
10. *St. Thomas and Epistemology.* Louis-Marie Regis, O.P. (1946) ISBN 0-87462-110-0
11. *St. Thomas and the Greek Moralists.* Vernon J.Bourke (1947) ISBN 0-87462-111-9
12. *History of Philosophy and Philosophical Education.* Étienne Gilson (1947) ISBN 0-87462-112-7
13. *The Natural Desire for God.* William R.O'Connor (1948) ISBN 0-87462-113-5
14. *St. Thomas and the World State.* Robert M. Hutchins (1949) ISBN 0-87462-114-3
15. *Method in Metaphysics.* Robert J. Henle, S.J. (1950) ISBN 0-87462-115-1
16. *Wisdom and Love in St. Thomas Aquinas.* Étienne Gilson (1951) ISBN 0-87462-116-X
17. *The Good in Existential Metaphysics.* Elizabeth G. Salmon (1952) ISBN 0-87462-117-8
18. *St. Thomas and the Object of Geometry.* Vincent E. Smith (1953) ISBN 0-87462-118-6

The Aquinas Lectures 1937–2023

The Aquinas Lectures 1937–2023

About the Aquinas Lecture Series

The Annual St. Thomas Aquinas Lecture Series began at Marquette University in the spring of 1937. Ideal for classroom use, library additions, or private collections, the Aquinas Lecture Series has received international prominence with scholars, universities, and libraries. Hardbound, uniform style; all volumes available, some reprints with soft covers.

Ordering information:
Marquette University Press
Phone: (800) 266-5564
Online: http://www.marquette.edu/mupress/

Editorial Address:
Marquette University Press
P.O. Box 3141
Milwaukee WI 53201-3141
Tel: (414) 288-1564